D1361083

FOLK COSTUME
OF SOUTHERN EUROPE

Hair dressing,
Candelaria in central Spain

Above: Costumes from Samugheo and Desulo, Sardinia
Opposite: Feast-day dress of Cercemaggiore, Molise, Italy

FOLK COSTUME
OF SOUTHERN EUROPE

LILLA M. FOX

Illustrated by the author

Publishers PLAYS, INC. *Boston*

Published in Great Britain by
Chatto & Windus Ltd

First American edition published by
PLAYS, INC. 1973

Library of Congress Catalog Card Number: 74-150101
ISBN: 0-8238-0088-1

Printed in Great Britain

Sunday dresses from Basle (left) and Valais

Contents

Peasant's cloak of Zamora region, Spain

*Fiesta dress,
huerta region of Murcia, Spain*

*Gold and silver brooch
from the Piedmont Alps*

*Halo bonnets worked in gold
from Gressoney in the Piedmont Alps*

Introduction

Folk costumes are rather like history books, for we can learn much about the past through being able to read them: a single costume could have sleeves fashionable in the court of one king, and a skirt from the court of another; a cap could be copied from caps worn by an invading army, jewellery perhaps brought home by a sailor from far away, and a special pattern of lace could have been invented in the village from which the costume originated.

The countries of Southern Europe that we are looking at in this book have known many wars and invasions. An early invasion was by Arab people, and although it was thirteen hundred years ago, Eastern fashions can still be seen in some folk costumes. The sash once worn by so many Spanish and Italian men is an Eastern fashion; it was useful as both belt and pocket, for into it a peasant could put anything from his dagger to his dinner.

In the Middle Ages, many fashions came from the Italian states. Cotton was grown there eight hundred years ago, and velvet made a hundred years later. "Venys Gold" from Venice was much prized; it was a decorative edging of gold threadwork, and is shown on the halo bonnet above, which is still worn for best in Gressoney in the Italian Alps. Gold and silver lace was made, and later on, lace of flaxen or cotton thread.

The Renaissance, which means re-birth, was a go-ahead time in the Italian states; in spite of much fighting, the states became rich and powerful, and people still crowd to see the beautiful cities that were built in those times. The clothes were magnificent, and the fashions spread to most European royal courts, and later to the country people. Italian peasants shared the prosperity, and they too dressed grandly until Sumptuary Laws stopped them. (Sumptuary Laws were intended to cut down extravagance in dress when the Church or State thought people were spending too much money on it, or dressing too finely for their place in society; some of these laws tried to dictate what each class of person should wear, and this is one reason why townspeople and peasants often wore different styles of costume. The effect of Sumptuary Laws never lasted long, especially among wealthy people!)

Other fashions followed. Spain became the most powerful country, occupying parts of Europe, and bringing the styles of the Spanish court: farthingales, stomachers, ruffs, and puffed-up sleeves and breeches. These fashions were followed by looser jackets and wide breeches, flowing dresses, and slit sleeves such as are still seen in Sardinia.

In the eighteenth century, France was the centre of fashion, with hoops and panniers, low-cut bodices, lots of lace, and decorative aprons; peasant women always wore aprons, but the ornamental best aprons, *not* suitable for cowsheds, date from this period. The long jackets, knee breeches and buckled shoes were adopted by the menfolk, and can be seen in many folk costumes today.

The Napoleonic Empire introduced the straight high-waisted Empire line, elaborate bonnets, patterned shawls from India and very short jackets. After this followed crinolines, more shawls, lace caps and frills, leg-o'-mutton sleeves, longer jackets, and long pants, top hats and trilbies, all of which have since become mixed up with other styles in various folk costumes.

Dancers from Ampezzo,
northern Italy

Look, for instance, at these costumes from Ampezzo in the Dolomite mountains in north-east Italy. Here the bodice is laced over a white chemise; the chemise has very full sleeves and the over-sleeve is tied on with an ornamental tie, an early Renaissance style. Then came the white fichu, the buckled shoes, and the flowered apron with its little bow in front, all of a later period, and finally the black stockings and the top hat, gaily decorated with a knot of flowers and two streamers. The man's costume dates from the eighteenth century, and the top hat is an even later fashion; the coloured waistcoat and neckerchief, the hat ornament and the large daisy buttons are both gay and special to Ampezzo.

Sun-hats from Portugal and Obwalden

Many people in Southern Europe are Catholics, and liked to dress up for Sundays and the Feast Days of the Church. Their clothes were as fine as they could make them; finery and jewellery were ways of showing how rich and important the wearer was. Southern Europe is a sunny part of the world so sun-hats are important, from workaday ones like this from Portugal to gay ones like the Sunday hat from Obwalden in Switzerland. There are many mountain ranges in Southern Europe, and that means rain, wind and snow; shepherds and cowherds had to wear tough breeches and gaiters and warm jackets as well as cloaks. In some places, rain-cloaks were made of straw like the one from Galicia in northern Spain. Apart from Switzerland, the countries in this book have long coastlines and busy fisheries; fishermen used to wear stocking-caps in different ways, as shown by the examples from Spain and Sardinia. As well as providing warmth, these caps were useful for putting things in, such as money.

Some of the costumes in this book, and many others for which there is no room, can only be seen in books or museums. Nowadays people have taken to wearing cheaper, factory-made clothes. Also, many country people have moved to industrial towns or to other countries, especially the United States; the old ways, the music and dancing, and

10

the costumes, are often forgotten (with one important exception, Switzerland, as we shall see later). In some places, however, especially in the mountains, folk costumes are still worn for special occasions, and you might see them on your travels. Folk-dancing groups are always careful to wear the right dress for their dances, usually making it themselves, and they visit abroad as well as dancing at home.

If you want costumes for a dance or play, try to make them as close to the original style as you can. Don't dress dancers of northern Spain in the flounces and mantillas of Andalucia, for instance; that would look as silly as bullfighters in evening dress! All these countries have Cultural Institutes in our country, where the people are friendly and helpful. Do not mix the costumes up, and call the result "national dress". There is really no such thing in Southern Europe, only many regional costumes, and most regions have enough different dresses to fill a book on their own.

Straw rain-cloak, Galicia

Spanish stocking-cap

Sardinian cap

Best Dress of Tiriolo, Calabria
Above: an embroidery pattern

1 Italy, South from Rome

A hundred years ago, when the Italian states joined to form one country, visitors could see a wonderful show of folk costumes. Peasants, townsfolk, fishermen and sailors, all wore their distinctive costumes, simple for work and grand for best. Even poorer peasants wore shirts and chemises of *bavalla*, a material made of the silk shreds left over from the weaving of the fine silks for which Italy was famous. Richer peasants wore best clothes of silk and velvet, with beautiful gold and silver jewellery. The men wore gold or silver buttons, gold earrings and brightly coloured silk sashes and neckerchiefs. All the clothes were made by the women out of hand-woven cloth made from hand-spun silk, cotton or fine wool, and the leather shoes as well as the *ciocce*, the working sandals, were hand-sewn, too.

If these visitors of a hundred years back had gone to the remote little town of Tiriolo in the Calabrian mountains in southern Italy, they would have seen the costume on the facing page: the bodice is laced over the chemise and the over-sleeve tied on at the shoulder, both early Renaissance styles; but both, as well as the white shawl and black head-kerchief, are made of lace, so that a once-simple style looks rich and ornate. The full, accordion-pleated skirt is worn straight or looped up to show the flowered lining, and the under-skirt is red with a striped or floral border, and worn over several petticoats. The wide striped stole, giving protection against the wind, has an Eastern look, and over everything the wearer has an array of necklaces, crosses, rosaries and pendants. If one could find out all the history of the Tiriolan costume, it would need a chapter to itself.

However, a hundred years ago most visitors went to Rome or Naples, and the costumes they saw in the surrounding country became well-known. In the mountain districts they would have seen men wearing working-clothes like those illustrated below: sheepskin jackets, wide breeches, leather gaiters and *ciocce*. The peasant women would have been dressed rather like the woman from Minturno, on the coast of the Lazio region between Rome and Naples, with her looped-up over-skirt, brocade bodice, and balloon sleeves made of closely pleated linen. (When such fine material was pleated, each pleat was sewn along its edge with tiny running-stitches.) Her headdress was a large white cloth, specially folded to give shade from the sun. Similar headdresses were worn in other parts of Italy, the size and way of folding the cloth varying from place to place. The headdress from Castel Madama, near Rome, is narrow and fastened with a jewelled pin.

Visitors to the south of Italy can still see the other well-known costume, the Neapolitan; it is similar to that worn by the Tarantella dancers of nearby Sorrento in Campania. The men wear breeches and stockings, full-sleeved shirts, red stocking-caps, and brightly coloured waistcoats, sashes and neckerchiefs. The girls wear laced bodices, white chemises with deep shoulder frills, and gaily coloured skirts and head-kerchiefs; red is a favourite colour.

Dancers from Sorrento

Peasant dress of Minturno, Lazio

Lazio peasant in working clothes

Pettorano sul Gizio, Abruzzi   Castel Madama, Lazio

Best dress of Pontelandolfo, near Benevento

Headdresses and a crucifix ring, a feature of the silver jewellery: Scanno, Abruzzi

Inland, in Benevento near Pontelandolfo at the foot of the Apennines, men's dress was like that of many other regions, a dark suit with knee breeches, white shirt, bright neckerchief and sash, and a round felt hat. The girls were almost hidden beneath their heavily fringed silk shawls, their jewellery, and their aprons woven with brilliant patterns; sleeves, tied on at the shoulder with embroidered ribbons, were made of four tiers of lace. Jewellery, including the huge earrings and sun pendant, the rosary and cross, was nearly all made of gold.

High in the Apennines, in the province of Abruzzi, is Scanno, where women still dress up on special occasions in dark dresses which show off their silver chains. A white cotton scarf is wound round the head over a pale blue ribbon that hangs in two streamers at the back. In the same region is Pettorano sul Gizio, where the huge white headcloth is surmounted by a tiny embroidered red one.

Bari, Apulia

Ruoti, Basilicata
The girl's sleeves are decorated with coins

Southward along the Adriatic coast is the region of Apulia, where some people still live in the stone beehive-shaped houses called *trulli*. In the coastal town of Bari, women wore stiff stomachers and pleated green silk aprons, and lacy headscarves. The men wore green sashes.

The countryfolk from Ruoti, in the region of Basilicata, might still be seen in their Sunday clothes. The woman's dress is dark, except for her white chemise with its finely pleated partlet, or square front; the girl has decorative braiding on her bodice and sleeves, and a white headdress.

Folk costume is still worn for best in parts of southern Italy; the dresses are handed down, being made of heavy homespun material, and with beautiful embroidery and hand-made lace. The skirts are often accordion-pleated, the pleats so close that they stand out from the body, the material so stiff and heavy that the pleats keep their shape. For everyday, many women still wear full black skirts with coloured bands according to their district; older women always wear black.

Pleats can be seen in this high-waisted dress from Spezzano, in the over-sleeves, the under-skirt, and the wide over-skirt pinned up in the front.

In the toe of Italy are the Aspromonte mountains, where men used to dress like this old *Zampognaro* (bagpiper) with loose breeches and soft leather sandals and a black stocking-cap folded to shade the eyes.

Sicily is often called "the garden of the Mediterranean". These dancers come from the hilly Madonie region; the man wears an embroidered and tasselled cap rather like a fez, and light clothes of gay colouring; the girl's skirt is made of strips of brightly patterned material.

*Bagpiper
(Zampognaro)
from the Aspromonte
mountains, Calabria*

Best dress of Spezzano, Calabria

Dancers from the Madonie region of Sicily

Sicily has always been a refuge for people fleeing from invaders or persecution. One such group were a party of Albanians who came there about five hundred years ago, and whose descendants still wear the old costume for special occasions. The men wear full-sleeved shirts, with embroidered waistcoats and sleeveless jackets; the trousers and tasselled cap are white and the cap has an embroidered, stiffened edge. The belt is made of gold wrought into patterns, and with a huge buckle carrying an image of a saint. Similar heavy gold belts are worn by the women. Their richly coloured dresses, ribbon headdresses and stiffened capes of coloured silks are embroidered in gold, and there is gold lace on the wide collars of their blouses. Sometimes, the women put on big mantillas, which almost hide their faces in the Eastern fashion.

Albanesi best dress, Sicily

Buttero from the Maremma, Tuscany

Old Genoese plaited lace

Peasant working dress of Emilia-Romagna

2   Italy, North from Rome

North of Rome are regions with historic cities and new industries, but where folk costume has died out. Only in the Maremma country, on the Tuscan coast, can herdsmen still be seen dressed like this *Buttero* (cowboy) with his spurred leather boots, and apron made of calf-skin fastened at the sides like the *chaparojos* of American cowboys. The girl beside him wears the pretty working clothes and coral beads which used to be worn in the Romagna district of Emilia.

Further north, the Apennine mountains slope down to the great plains of Piedmont and Lombardy; northwards still and to the west rise the Alps, and in their upland valleys are remnants of a rich tradition of folk costume and customs. The Valli de Lanza lies in the Piedmont Alps between Turin and France, and here folk costume was worn for best until recently.

The costume illustrated has a French look, with its elegant dark silk dress, and apron decorated with black lace, in contrast to the big white headdress, which is made of starched lace bound round with a wide, lacy ribbon.

The Val d'Aosta is high up in the northern Alps. Gressoney is in this region, the main characteristics of its folk costume being the gold bonnet and jewellery shown on page 7, and so is Cogne, where until lately old women could be seen at work in the fields dressed as the illustration opposite shows. The dress is high-waisted and full, and the apron like an over-skirt; the chemise has a wide ruff. The necklace would have been of real coral, which was highly prized by peasants in many countries.

Further west, in the mountain town of Fobello, best dress was black. The over-skirt was turned up, and squares of embroidery on its underside matched the embroidery on the bodice; there was more embroidery on the partlet, and on the shoulders and high collar of the blouse. The black stockings were worn full at the ankle, and decorated with lines of colour.

The old couple come from Sondrio in the Valtellina region of Lombardy. The man wears black with a red waistcoat, and his wife is also in black with a red headkerchief and blouse, and a dark blue apron. Brianza is a region south of Lake Como, also in Lombardy; here, women's costume was light and pretty. The headdress was a halo of silver *spillone* (hairpins) on a wired framework, held in place by two filigree silver pins.

Bonnet from Cogne

Best dress of
Valli de Lanza, Piedmont Alps

Peasant dress
of Cogne, Val d'Aosta

Feast-day dress
of Fobello, Piedmont Alps

Brianza, Lombardy

Sondrio, Valtellina, Lombardy

Costumes from
Val di Gardena
in the Alto Adige
The girls are dressed
for the Easter festival

In the Val di Gardena in the Dolomite mountains, folk costumes are still worn on special occasions. Married women wear high black felt or woollen caps over lace *coifs* (undercaps) and big silk aprons tied with blue ribbon, with a bow of embroidered ribbon in the front. Girls wear big lace aprons and their white chemises have lace ruffs and cuffs. Bodices, red and green, are laced over yellow *plastrons* (triangular panels, usually stiffened and embroidered, worn in front of the bodice or just inside it). The headdress is made of red brocade ribbon fixed on a black velvet band which is tied in a big bow at the back; a halo of pointed silver *spillone* surrounds the bun, and on top of the head is a crown of lace and a topknot of flowers.

Eastward in the Friuli region is Ampezzo, whose folk costume is illustrated on page 9.

All these costumes and many more would have been worn a hundred years ago; now only a few can be seen on their rightful wearers. Fortunately, there are folk-dancing groups who still wear the costumes of their regions; one of these is the group from Aviano on the edge of the mountains in Friuli, from whose gay dress the last picture is copied.

Aviano folk dancers

Headdresses based on historical styles

Basle   *Geneva*

3   Switzerland I

Switzerland is formed from a number of regions or *cantons*; each canton is self-governing, and has its own customs, traditions and folk costumes, and within many of the cantons are valleys and upland villages with still more traditions and costumes. In the seventeenth and eighteenth centuries certain places became known for their industries, such as Zurich for silk, Basle for ribbons and braids, and Appenzell for embroidery. These were made mainly to sell, but the work-people took some into their own dress, making it gay and colourful.

For many years visitors were few because of the difficult mountain passes which had to be crossed, but when railway tunnels were cut, Switzerland became a very popular holiday place; the old ways of life changed quickly, and folk costume started to go out of fashion. Many Swiss people were sad to see old customs being forgotten, and in 1926 they started a League to keep them alive. Thanks to this, a number of the old festivals are still celebrated, and the folk costumes—instead of dying out as in so many other countries—are in certain places worn for everyday as well as for best. Some have been redesigned to make them more practical. In other places, people have copied ideas for dress from old pictures, like the ladies from Basle and Geneva shown at the head of this chapter. Old skills of weaving, embroidery, leather and metal-work have been revived, too.

Uri is one of the three Forest Cantons that first joined together in 1291, and has the oldest folk costume. The upland farmer wears a hooded working smock called a *sayon*, and sandals called *socques*, like the Italian *ciocce* but with shaped wooden soles that give a firm foothold in all weathers. On Sunday he wears an embroidered blue smock. Smocks are one of the oldest types of dress, originating in the Saxon *smoca*. The farmer's wife wears a bodice laced over an embroidered plastron, a silk brocade apron and fichu, lacy mittens and full short sleeves—a common Swiss summer style. Her little cap is made of yards of black ribbon pleated and sewn on a wire framework surrounding a tiny lace coif. The old custom of black lace headdresses for girls, and white for married women, survives in Canton Uri. The girl wears a jewelled pin in her hair, known in Switzerland as *une flèche* (an arrow).

Working smock or sayon

Sunday dress of Canton Uri

The flèche

Wooden-soled socque

Married woman and girl

Costumes from Einsiedeln, Schwyz

Working clothes

*Sunday dress with
butterfly headdress*

*Girls' black lace cap
with double-headed flèche*

The farmer's wife from Einsiedeln wears a gingham working-dress, but on Sundays she, like other women in Canton Schwyz, wears silk brocade with an embroidered fichu, white lace mittens and a "fall" of lace from her sleeves. Her butterfly cap is made of flowers and gold lace with white lace wings stiffened with wire; single girls wear a halo cap of black lace and a double-headed *flèche*. The farmer wears a strong leather belt over his white working-smock.

In the Nidwalder region of the third Forest Canton, Unterwalden, Sunday clothes are grand. The man's short smock and his wife's blue bodice are embroidered; her full sleeves are pleated, and in her hair a *flèche* holds together an arrangement of plaits covered in red ribbon. This costume has an attractive feature, seen elsewhere in Switzerland: the silver chains hung between silver filigree "tulips" or "roses" on the front and back of the bodice. The more chains there are, the richer the wearer. Necklets are typical of this region, both the gold one worn over a black band, and the old lady's strands of coral fastened to gold plaques. She also wears a "mirror" silver hair ornament.

*Front of bodice showing
filigree rose and tulip ornaments*

Silver "mirror" hair ornament

Sunday dress of Nidwalder, Unterwalden

Sunday dress of Canton Lucerne

This feast-day costume is typical of Canton Lucerne: a brocade bodice, embroidered plastron, full sleeves, and a lace partlet with a finely goffered frill (goffering was done with hot goffering irons, like long scissors with thin bars instead of blades). The pleated skirt is woven with bands of colour which vary from village to village. The bonnet is made of black horsehair lace, and the sun-hat carries two flat bows and two knots of flowers.

In Cantons Zurich and St Gallen, halo or wheel coifs are often seen. One example, a wire framework embroidered in gold or silver thread, with a bow at the back, comes from St Gallen, and the other, a huge wheel of black lace, comes from Uznach.

St Gallen, with another design in gold

Wheel headdresses

Uznach

Uznach

St Gallen

Klettgau bonnet

*Workaday (above)
and Sunday caps
from Moutier, Jura*

Sunday dress of Klettgau, Schaffhausen

Sunday dress of Delémont, Jura

In Protestant areas the dress is usually more sober, such as this woman's costume from Klettgau in Canton Schaffhausen, where the style has not changed since 1793. Women wear black with simply embroidered plastrons and striped hand-woven aprons, and either a little *beguin* (bonnet) or toque.

Further west is the long Canton Berne, stretching from the Jura mountains to the Bernese Oberland. In the Jura region, lace caps are worn; two are shown, one from Moutier, and another from Delémont, with a simple dress. The men's Sunday smocks are blue, embroidered in white.

Embroidery motif from Argovie Bernoise

Sunday dress of Emmental

Workaday dress of Gruyères

In Emmental, near the city of Berne, the costume is gayer, with its yellow plastron and partlet, very full skirt with a band of colour, striped apron and silver chains; the bright colours are shown up by the bands of black velvet on the bodice and partlet. The yellow hat, stiffened with sulphur, is called a *Schwefelhut*; the *beguin* has a black horsehair lace frill.

Gruyères, famous for its cheese, lies in the mountains of Canton Fribourg; here, the men wear a dark jacket with balloon sleeves, called a *bredzon*, embroidered with edelweiss. The black leather *loï*—a bag containing salt for the cows to lick—is suitably embroidered too. A coloured belt and black capette are also worn, and for best a shirt with full sleeves in fine concertina pleats. Heavy brown jackets are worn in winter, knitted in a variety of local patterns. The stripes on the women's aprons also vary from place to place. The cow in the illustration wears its folk costume, an embroidered collar and a very large bell.

Westward lie Cantons Vaud and Neuchâtel, where the women wear straw hats; many are like this big yellow *chapeau à borne* with its "chimney" on top. Hat and apron are tied with yellow ribbon. The wearer comes from Montreux at the eastern end of Lake Geneva, and the country girl on the right from Neuchâtel.

Sun-hats from Montreux and Neuchâtel

St Maurice

Val d'Anniviers

Folk costume from Valais

Group from Evolène in Sunday dress

4 Switzerland II

Canton Valais is a long mountainous region and every valley has a distinguishing feature of dress. Hats and bonnets are decorated with different arrangements of ribbons; women used to spend a lot of time and money on these ribbons, and the deeper the pleats, the more important and wealthy was the wearer. Sober-coloured ribbons were worn for Sunday, and black for mourning; violet and silver were worn for Advent and Lent, red and gold for Whitsun and the anniversaries of martyred Saints, and for the most important occasions—Christmas, Easter, christenings, first communions or weddings—ribbons of white and gold. The two hats illustrated are from St Maurice and the Val d'Anniviers. Another can be seen at Evolène, worn with a long-sleeved dress and a red and white fichu; the best dress which the child wears could be red or blue, with bands of embroidery.

The women of Valais, like country-women everywhere, were quick to adopt into their own costume any fashion that took their fancy. An example of this is the little top hat ornamented with gold braid and worn over a lace coif by the girl from Sion, a town in the Rhône valley; her bodice and sleeves are also decorated with gold braid.

Sunday dress of Sion, Valais

Canton Ticino stretches from the Alps to Lakes San Maggiore and Lugano. Costumes here are Italian in style, like the brocade dress from Mendrisio with tied-on over-sleeves, and a headdress made of twenty-four *spillone*, held in place by two silver arrows and a double-headed pin. The wooden-soled sandals are called *zocolli*.

Mendrisio, Ticino

Eastward, the Alps stretch to the borders of Austria and to the Engadine mountains in Canton Grisons. Typical of this once very remote region are the little *capadüsli* (caps), such as these from the Davos and Prätigau valleys, which are made from the same hand-woven fabric as the jackets, and edged with lace. A tiny *capadüsli* is worn by the woman from the High Engadine in her red dress with its finely pleated skirt. Her *capadüsli* and fichu are decorated with gold lace, and the bold flower patterns on her fichu and bodice are embroidered in gold thread. She wears a lace collar called a *murinella* and amber beads; the whole costume is very dignified.

Northward through Canton St Gallen, we come to little Canton Appenzell with its two districts, Ausser and Inner Rhoden and their splendid costumes. Here, cowherds are important people, and there are annual dances and festivals connected with their work. For

Capadüsli from Prätigau and Davos (below)

Embroidery motif from Prätigau

Everyday beguin or cap, Ausser Rhoden

Best dress of the High Engadine

Festival and best dress from Ausser Rhoden

these the cowherds wear scarlet waistcoats and soft leather breeches, little caps or black hats decorated with flowers. A coloured kerchief is draped over the left hip. The waistcoat is embroidered with white flowers, and the leather braces decorated with an appliqué pattern of cows. A brooch at the neck, a single earring and silver watch-chains complete the costume (see also page 37). The women wear black silk bodices with stiffened fronts and little insets of silk to match the aprons. The wings of the butterfly headdresses are made of wired black tulle— a kind of muslin—lined with white lace and fixed to a little *beguin* with a bow at the back. The enormous cowbells are slung on wide collar-straps with big gilded buckles, woven in red and yellow. The group above comes from Ausser Rhoden.

Filigree silver attachments
for bodice and shoulder chains

Festival dress from Inner Rhoden

The best dress from Inner Rhoden is magnificent, and can be seen in
all its glory at church festivals. The skirt, although full and pleated in
accordion pleats, is woven from very fine wool and does not stick out,
as so many peasant skirts do, but falls straight to make the wearer look
tall and elegant. The long-sleeved jacket matches the skirt and has a
wide double collar of goffered lace, while the deep cuff is decorated
with white and black lace. The finely pleated apron is silk, and so is the
blouse under the pointed bodice. The bodice lacing is fastened to

filigree silver roses and many silver chains and necklaces are worn. The big butterfly headdress is called the *Schlappe*: on the head is a little cap made of gold lace, called the *bonet d'or*, with a large bow at the back, and over the ears are two "roses" made of pleated black ribbon. Between the *bonet d'or* and the roses are fixed big wings, made of wired black tulle and lined with white goffered lace folding outwards into two points at the front. This is the headdress of married women; girls do not wear ribbons or white lace, but flowers over their foreheads instead.

We have toured Switzerland, leaving out many of the cantons and their costumes. But those who visit Switzerland have a good chance of seeing some Swiss folk costumes, thanks to the League formed in 1926, and to the skill and artistry of the people who make and wear them.

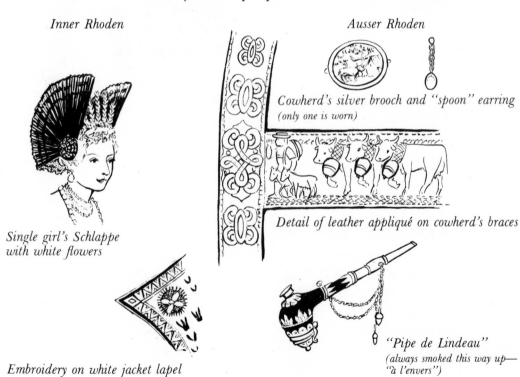

Inner Rhoden

Ausser Rhoden

Cowherd's silver brooch and "spoon" earring
(only one is worn)

Single girl's Schlappe with white flowers

Detail of leather appliqué on cowherd's braces

Embroidery on white jacket lapel

"Pipe de Lindeau"
(always smoked this way up—
"à l'envers")

Sardinian fiesta costumes

Teulada

Oliena

5   The Mediterranean Islands: Sardinia, Corsica, Malta and the Balearic Islands

These islands have been conquered many times, and their conquerors have brought new customs as well as styles of dress. However, the islanders have often gone their own way in spite of this, and kept some of their old ways and costumes. The Sardinians are the most independent of all (in Roman times, Sards were very unmanageable slaves!) and their individuality shows in their striking folk costumes. At one time every village had its own dress, and some can still be seen at the annual festival of folk dance and costume at Cagliari.

The couple above come from Teulada in the south; like many Sardinians, the man wears black and white, with wooden-soled boots and a big black stocking-cap over a skull cap, usually black too, but here embroidered; he has a stand-up collar and silver buttons. The woman wears a pleated skirt and a contrasting apron; the shape, size and decoration of aprons differed from village to village, so one could always tell where the wearer came from. Her headkerchief is of white lace, and is sometimes worn beneath a coloured mantilla. (The word mantilla means "little cloak": these can vary in size, but are always rounded at the back. Headkerchiefs and shawls are made of material folded crosswise, so that they fall in a point behind.)

Sleeves in Sardinia are very full, and the jacket sleeves are often slashed to show the white under-sleeve. In Oliena red jackets are edged with bands of green embroidery. The men wear short black kilts called *ragas*, and decorated belts. Their shirts and the women's pleated chemises are fastened with filigree gold buttons.

The dress from Sennori in the north shows elaborate embroidery, and the skirt is finely pleated. The headdress is made of a long piece of material wound round head and neck to form a wimple, with the end starched and folded over to act as a sun-hat. Other Sardinian costumes from the central mountain regions can be seen in the frontispiece.

Fiesta dress of Sennori

Sleeve from Itturi, Sennori

Left: Corsican shepherd and his wife

Right: Maltese lady wearing a faldetta

Corsica is now part of France, but most Corsicans speak a dialect of Italian. They keep very much to themselves, especially those who live among the mountains. Their costumes were simple and always black, except for the *marezzo*, the headkerchief, which was often coloured.

To the south is Malta, whose people were more influenced by Eastern ways. About two hundred years ago, women were veiled, and the only remaining bit of folk costume, the *faldetta*, is a sort of veil. It was once a skirt worn over the head; the waistband makes a long stiffened brim, one end held in the hand, the other floating free. Visitors have likened Maltese women in their *faldettas* to ships in full sail.

The Balearic islands, Majorca, Minorca and Ibiza, are Spanish, the islanders being mostly of Catalonian stock. Now they are holiday places, and folk costume is rarely worn except to please tourists. Fiesta dress in Majorca was made of flowered brocade and lace, with a big mantilla and, under the chin, a little fan-pleated ruffle. Working dress was black with a cloth pinned round as an apron over the skirt, both made of striped hand-woven material. The men wore Eastern-style sashes and full white breeches, with black sombreros over head-kerchiefs; all their clothes were coloured, either plain, striped, checked or with small patterns.

Women's fiesta dress in Ibiza was bright and varied, with coloured aprons, silk headkerchiefs and long-frilled shawls. Most important was the array of gold chains and necklaces worn across the front; these were precious heirlooms and indicated the wealth of the wearer. The men wore stocking-caps, and everyone wore *alpargatos*, the rope-soled canvas shoes so common in Spain and southern France; the men's were laced with black over white stockings, and the girls' had white laces over black stockings.

Servant girl

Fiesta dress from Majorca and Ibiza

Fiesta costume of Valencia

*Combs with
dangling ornaments*

6 Spain I

To most people Spain means bullfighting, *señoritas*, and sunny holidays. This is only a very small part of the picture, and it is not along the holiday coast that the most vivid costumes were to be found. Valencia is on this coast, however, and the Valencian costume is the prettiest, with its fine lace and flowery-patterned silk in delicate shades of colour. Valencian lace and silk have long been famous, and the fiesta costumes show both to advantage. The women's hair was done in the style of eastern Spain, plaited and wound into "earphones", with high buns or chignons at the back, and decorated with silver hairpins and jewelled pins and combs. Jewelled ornaments dangle from the haircomb of the Valencian lady shown above; this is an Arab style of decoration, and reminds us that Spain was for long an Arab kingdom. When it broke up into a number of independent, smaller Spanish kingdoms— to be united in the fifteenth century under one king—some Arab craftsmen and their families continued to live and work in various parts of Spain long afterwards. In a very few places the skills they taught are still used, and some of their old traditions have been maintained.

Arab influence can be seen in many folk costumes, too, such as men's costume from the *huerta* (fruit-growing) districts. The man shown on page 6 wears a wide violet-coloured sash over full white shorts called *carguells*, a word from Arabic; his headkerchief is wound round like a turban, and his silk waistcoat and *espardenyes* (rope-soled sandals) are yellow. Such costumes were worn at fiestas early in this century, but it is unlikely you would see them unless worn by a folk-dancing group. The same is true of most Spanish costume.

Northward from Valencia is Catalonia, a region with its own language and traditions. Fishing has always been an important industry, so it is not surprising to find that at one time both men and women wore long dangling fish-nets on their heads as well as their caps and headkerchiefs. Otherwise, their fiesta costumes were simple: for men, a dark home-spun suit with silver buttons, a coloured silk or velvet waistcoat, a sash, *alpargatos* (Catalonian rope-soled sandals) and a red stocking-cap; for women, shot-silk skirts, usually red, black bodices, and black lace aprons and mittens. The ends of the headkerchief were crossed behind the head and tied on top.

Catalonian dance dress

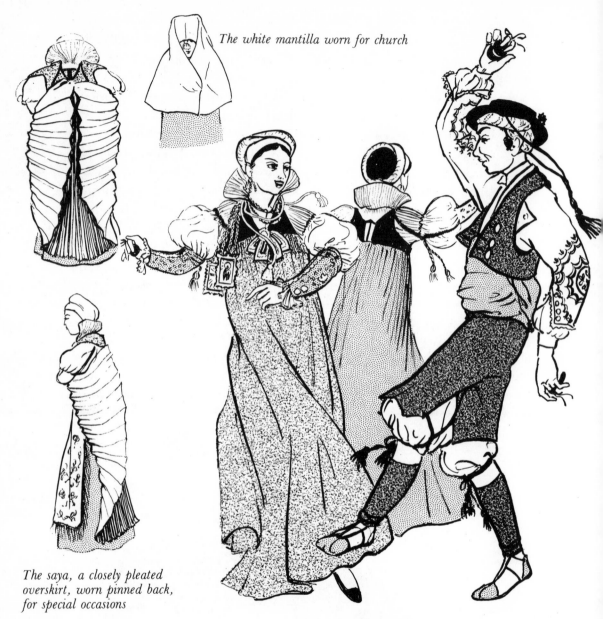

The white mantilla worn for church

The saya, a closely pleated
overskirt, worn pinned back,
for special occasions

Fiesta costume of Ansó

In the high mountain region of Aragon, there was once great variety of costume. Those from the Ansó valley are particularly old and unusual; the women's long flowing skirts are called *basquinas*, as similar skirts were once worn by Basque women. Until a girl was twelve, she would wear a red *basquina*; the green one she would then be given was often handed down within the family from generation to generation. (It was said that a new *basquina*, being woven from heavy homespun wool, would outlive its wearer.) Black *basquinas* were worn for church.

The skirt is gathered into a tiny yoke, the armholes bound in red, the neck in yellow. The chemise has very full sleeves and a finely pleated collar that stands up rather like the seventeenth-century Spanish collar, the *golilla*. The over-sleeves are brightly coloured and fastened to tasselled red and yellow bands tied just below the shoulders. A *scapular* hung from the right shoulder; this was a holy picture or relic suspended on brightly embroidered ribbons. On special occasions, a *sofacanta* was also worn—a big bow with many loops of red, pink and white ribbons —a gold pendant, and the image of a saint. As often in Spain, women wore a number of gold chains and necklaces with rosaries, crosses and ornamental reliquaries: little caskets containing sacred relics.

Although the headdress looks like a turban, it is really two plaits bound with coloured material and pinned round the head with a band of material running across the forehead. Sometimes a white cap was worn over this, or a big mantilla to match the *basquina*. Often the man-tilla had a *tufa*—a tassel—in front; older women usually wore this type of head-covering. The men wore full-sleeved shirts and full white breeches, and over them dark waistcoats and jackets, coloured sashes, and wide short breeches slit at the sides and sometimes tied to a tasselled knee-band. Over red headkerchiefs, small black hats were worn, from which hung two cords twisted together to make a tassel at the end. The men wore either boots or *alpargatos* like the women, or very primitive sandals called *albarcas*.

Westward through Navarre we come to the Basque country on the Bay of Biscay. The couple below from Pamplona are folk dancers in fiesta dress. The woman wears a red skirt looped up over her dark accordion-pleated under-skirt, a long-sleeved bodice and a lacy head-kerchief. The man wears a dark suit with a long loose jacket which has wide sleeves slit to the elbow, and over it a big pleated white collar, reminiscent of seventeenth-century costume. He wears the little pom-pom tie and round black hat with streamers which are seen so often in the French Pyrenees and remind us that the Basques, a people whose language is probably the oldest in Europe, were divided between France and Spain.

Dancers from Pamplona

Dancers from Asturias

Further west along the coast is the rainy, hard-working region of Asturias where folk costumes were more simple and sober in colour. Nevertheless, fiesta dress, now worn only by folk dancers, was cheerful: the women's skirts were edged with black, the men's red sashes and red-fronted waistcoats patterned on the back. The little embroidered aprons and headkerchiefs were often brightly coloured and so were the small lace-edged capes with long ends pinned behind the wearer.

The old kingdom of Galicia lies in the north-west corner of Spain. The fiesta dress of the town of Muros had a fitted bodice and full-sleeved short jacket of brocade, and a velvet-edged cape with ends to tie at the back. The skirt was made of stiff homespun fabric, and cut in a flare, narrow at the top and very wide at the hem, which gave it a hooped effect. The headdress, or *cofia*, was made of embroidered white muslin and lace, and tied with ribbons—red for a girl, white for a wife, and black for a widow.

Galicia is rich in folksong and dance, and there were many occasions for wearing these fiesta costumes. The boy below wears a full-sleeved linen shirt, and red flannel-fronted waistcoat embroidered in blue, green and yellow; his gaiters are black with red piping and tassel at the toe; the coat is carried over the left shoulder. His hat, or *monteira*, is made of coloured velvet trimmed with contrasting cord and tufts; the long sidepiece is called the "Listening Piece". The girl wears a full red dress with black velvet bands, a black velvet apron trimmed with jet and black lace, and a big brightly coloured shawl over a red woollen cape, which is also decorated with black velvet and jet.

Bodice and jacket

Muros

Fiesta costume from Galicia

Detail of a button

Turégano, Segovia

7   Spain II

The central regions of Spain are high, with jagged mountain ranges and wide plateaux, cold in the winter and hot and dusty in the summer. Fiesta costumes are especially striking and carry reminders of the court life of bygone kings as well as old Arabian skills in gold and silver-work. The brilliant dresses of the women are set off by the dark clothes of the men, usually made from brown homespun cloth. Early in this century, some folk costumes were still worn for everyday as well as for fiestas.

In Turégano in the Segovia region, men wore large black sombreros, and heavy cloaks to protect them from the cold dry winds; the white under-breeches and stockings and the coloured sashes contrast with the darker garments, and the tassels, gold earring, and gold or silver buttons on men's clothes, often had very long shanks. The women could protect themselves from the wind by folding their gathered or pleated skirts over their heads; their shawls were flower-patterned and their aprons striped.

Many of the necklaces and chains worn at fiesta-time carry crosses, reliquaries and medallions with pictures of saints, as well as pagan charms and amulets. The most splendid necklaces could be seen in La Alberca in Salamanca; some of these were made of huge gold beads decorated in a manner taught by Arab craftsmen, and worn on top of many other necklaces, almost hiding the dress beneath. This had a wide heavy skirt decorated with striking braiding; there were patterns in gold braid on the sleeves and big gold buttons on the jacket. The long, lacy embroidered scarf is worn with one end fastened low over the forehead, and the rest wound round the head so hiding most of the face, in Eastern style. Men's dress was striking, too: a black velvet suit with large silver buttons.

Detail of beads

Fiesta costume of La Alberca

Pendant and
beaded embroidery
from the Charros region,
Salamanca (see cover)

Fiesta costume of Avila

In Avila, one of the highest regions, women used to wear this fiesta costume. Over a full skirt worn with many petticoats is a white apron decorated with special embroidery called "Spanish Blackwork". The woman has on a black jacket and a shawl with brilliantly coloured flowers against a dark background, and over her head a mantilla which could be pinned up round her hat. The straw hat would have been made and decorated by its wearer with straw braids, crystals, ribbons and a mirror—a very old custom which was supposed to keep away evil spirits; the spirit saw itself in the mirror, mistook itself for another spirit, took fright, and ran away!

Embroidered chemise
and gorguera

Fiesta dress of Lagartera

Lagartera, in the long Toledo valley, was once a centre of the silk-worm industry and also famous for embroidery; the fiesta costume shows both these to advantage. The full skirt was accordion-pleated, the pleats standing out from the body and held together by stitching and bands of lace; it was worn over eight petticoats, each one a different colour. The silk chemise was embroidered with black and honey-coloured thread at the neck and wrists or elbows, and an over-chemise, the *gorguera*, was also worked in black. The gathered apron was embroidered and decorated with braiding, the embroidered shawl edged with lace, and the footless stockings embroidered in silk. The dress had a great show of brocade and ribbons, often edged with silver lace; there was a bow on the head, and several streamers were fastened at the back of the silk-embroidered girdle. Coral and gold filigree beads were worn as well as a rosary with a medallion of the Virgin, patroness of Toledo. On special occasions, a posy of silken leaves, flowers and fruit would be added.

Everyday clothes were simple, and more sober in colouring. The mother in the drawing below wears a plain fichu over her chemise and accordion-pleated skirt, and the baby a hand-made lace dress and a cape decorated with ribbons. The grandfather wears a smock, and the father's white woollen waistcoat with its blue neckband, typical of this region, was usually worn over a linen shirt. Young girls used to embroider best shirts for their sweethearts, with white linen thread.

Earring and pendant

Bead embroidery and silver lace

Family from Lagartera in everyday costume

Part of a skirt with braiding embroidered and ruched ribbons, and silver lace

Hairstyle and earring

Fiesta costume of Montehermosa, Estremadura

*The gorra, as worn by
single (left) and married women*

Montehermosa is on the western edge of the mountains of central Spain, and here fiesta costumes were dramatic and colourful. Men wore dark brown suits with sashes and homespun linen shirts embroidered in white at the cuffs and on the shirt-front. Their white cotton stockings were knitted in a raised pattern, and breeches, garters and sombreros were all decorated with tassels.

Women wore closely pleated short skirts made of stiff homespun fabric over several petticoats, and short jackets with big embroidered turnback cuffs; their cross-over capes were decorated with rosettes of red ribbon, and two pairs of richly embroidered streamers hung from the back of the waistband. The brocaded silk headkerchiefs, usually maroon in colour, had one end thrown up over the topknot of hair. Above this came the *gorra*—a high-crowned straw bonnet similar to those fashionable in Napoleon's Paris, and said to have been copied from one made by a milliner in a nearby town; it was worn tilted forward, with the high crown right on top of the head, and decorated with straw braids and plaits, ribbons, crystals and a mirror. Unmarried girls made and decorated their own *gorras*; when they married they wore the simpler *gorra* of a wife. For everyday, *gorras* were worn with a plainer version of the dress, usually maroon-coloured too.

In the remote western region of Estremadura, the character of the land, the way of life, and the costumes alter. Cattle, sheep and horses are herded, and practical leather clothes are needed. However, these were often elaborately decorated, and the same love of adornment can still be seen on the harnesses and trappings of horses and carts.

The shepherd from the pasturelands of the Cáceres region wears a *zamarro*, a sheepskin tabard described as early as 1611, shaped at the back to give protection from the wind, and edged with goatskin. He wears *zahones*—a half-leg covering of leather strapped to each thigh, like the *chaparajos* of the American cowboy—and carries a leather bag and horn drinking-cup. *Zahones* were often decorated with appliquéd

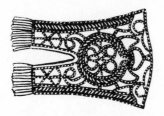

Appliqué leather decoration on zahones, Estremadura

and worked leather. Reddish goatskin is used for appliqué patterns, and also to edge the breeches of the herdsmen from Badajoz in the southern part of the region; they wear broad sashes and elaborately decorated leggings, and the number of steel buttons worn on the cuffs is a mark of rank.

The girl from Campanario, in southern Estremadura, wears a skirt hand-woven with many coloured stripes according to her district—and to the taste of the wearer, since she would have woven it herself. Each also embroidered her black apron, and decorated her hanging-pocket with leather openwork over coloured satin. Stockings were knitted in variously coloured patterns.

Shepherd from Cáceres   *Herdsman from Badajoz*   *Girl from Campanario*

Haircomb

Andalucian fiesta costume

Andalucia was once the richest part of Arab Spain, and Eastern influence lingers on in buildings and customs: older women still can be seen wearing big black mantillas folded across their faces. In contrast, the flounces and lace mantillas of Andalucian fiesta costume look showy. Mantillas are usually draped over a high comb, and are worn black for going to church, and white for going to bullfights—"for the bull," it is said. The girl in this picture is partnered by an elegant young man in a dark suit with a bright sash, white gaiters and a straight-brimmed Cordova hat; he is most probably an expert horseman, as horses are very popular in Andalucia.

Andalucia is also the home of the wild, long-horned cattle whose bulls are so formidable in the ring. The herdsmen of the upland ranches wear dark green dress and hats with rolled-up brims, while those of the plain wear black or grey and have Cordova hats, shown below. Both wear *zahones*, often appliquéd round the edges, and spurred leather boots. The fierce and hardy Andalucian cattle were the first to be taken to the New World, and with them went the tough Arab horses and indomitable herdsmen who became the first cowboys of America.

Andalucian herdsmen

Embroidery motif and filigree earring from Minho

Campino fiesta dress

8 Portugal

When the old kingdoms of Spain joined together under one king, Portugal remained independent. Tough and hard-working, the Portuguese built up their own country, and established an empire in the New World. Like the Spanish, they took their cattle across the Atlantic, and with them went the *Campinos*, the Portuguese cowboys. Illustrated at the head of this chapter is the *Campino* fiesta costume: breeches, a scarlet-fronted waistcoat with a patterned back, a short jacket carried over the left shoulder, and a green stocking-cap, the *barrete verd*. The *Campinos* wore *zahones* for work, the women black-banded red skirts over many starched white petticoats, white knee-length stockings, and gold chains to show off their wealth.

Fishing is an important industry, and fish porters and travelling fishmongers wear tin hats, with gutter brims to catch the drips from the wet fish (see page 61). Women workers both inland and on the quays—women have always worked very hard in Portugal—carry burdens on a round pad on their heads; the mother carries her baby as well as vegetables in her home-made basket. In the ports of Leiria and Oporto women used to wear headdresses similar to those of Bedouin women—little round hats over loose flowing kerchiefs.

Minho folk dancers

The most beautiful costume in Portugal comes from Viana do Castello in the Minho district. Here the full skirt was made of striped homespun linen; the chief colour was red, but the colouring and arrangement of stripes differed with every girl, since each wove her own. Broad red or black bands showed from which village the wearer came. The chemise was embroidered with a special blue floral pattern at the neck, shoulders and cuffs, and over it a bodice was worn, made in two sections, usually red above and black beneath, but sometimes pale blue, purple or olive green; it was embroidered with sequins and coloured wool. The aprons were so thickly woven with flower patterns that they felt like carpets, and on the gathers at the waist each girl might embroider her name, or that of her village, or perhaps a word like *Amor* (love). The hanging-pocket was always embroidered too. The red headkerchief could be tied in a variety of ways. The white knee-length and often footless stockings were knitted in lacy patterns, and high leather wooden-soled boots or mules were worn over them; the word *mule*, meaning a slip-on shoe, is Portuguese. On special occasions, they were replaced by leather-soled *mules* with finely embroidered uppers. The girls also liked to wear a lot of gold jewellery—chains, crosses, earrings and heart-shaped pendants.

The men's black suits and tasselled sombreros contrasted well with this finery; they wore red, too, with red jacket linings and sashes, and red and black embroidery on their shirts. Their silver buttons were always sewn on in a curve.

The Portuguese are justly proud of the Minho costume, and it is still made and worn by folk dancers and for fiestas.

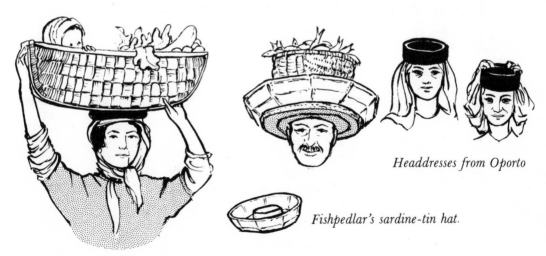

Headdresses from Oporto

Fishpedlar's sardine-tin hat.

Peasant woman with basket

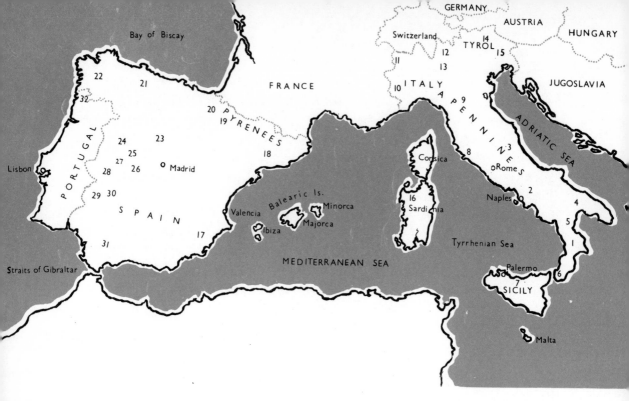

Key to Map

The numbers before the items refer to those on the map. The numbers after them are page references. Italic figures refer to illustrations.

Key to Map of Swiss Cantons

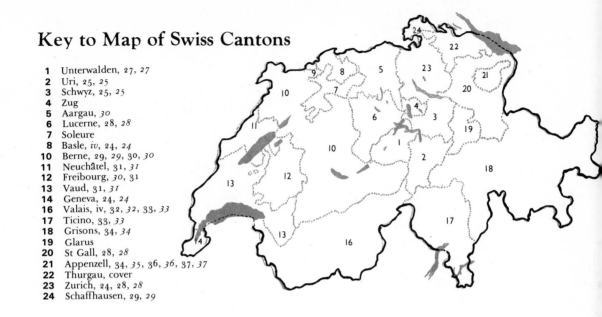

Index

64